Aleutian Incidents: Journal of PVT Robert A. Allen 1943-1944

Jeff Kreifels

Published by Jeff Kreifels, 2024.

While every precaution has been taken in the preparation of this book, the publisher assumes no responsibility for errors or omissions, or for damages resulting from the use of the information contained herein.

ALEUTIAN INCIDENTS: JOURNAL OF PVT ROBERT A. ALLEN 1943-1944

First edition. June 21, 2024.

Copyright © 2024 Jeff Kreifels.

Written by Jeff Kreifels.

Preface

My Aunt, Cathleen Cardinal, passed away in 2022, after living in the same house in Shelton, Washington, all of her life. Her mother (my grandmother), Dorothy Cardinal who passed away in 2017 at the age of 102, purchased that house in the early 1940s. Dorothy's grandfather, Daniel Keelty, was a Shelton pioneer, moving to Shelton in the 1880s. This house, occupied by mother & daughter for about 80 years, became a repository for local and family history.

In the process of cleaning out Cathleen Cardinal's house after she passed away, I was fascinated with all of the "history" I was finding. At the time, I was a high school history teacher. I separated out pictures, letters, documents & artifacts that to me had some historical value (intrinsic value for recording, understanding, and sharing of what happened), into boxes of "to explore later." Later came in 2023 as I retired from teaching. Now, with time on my hands and decades of having a personal passion for exploring and teaching history, I had the opportunity to go through the 100 year old photo albums and 80 year old pictures that I had uncovered in the house.

One treasure that I found fascinating was a handwritten journal by Robert A. Allen. He was my great uncle. I never knew him nor had I heard anything of him, except for minor details in the family tree. Robert A. Allen, 1906-1963, brother to Dorothy Cardinal (Allen). As I began reading his journal, I was drawn by the simplicity, the attention to detail, the everyday experience of this WWII soldier. His journal was written about his deployment in Alaska from July 1943 to September 1944. I felt like I was experiencing life in Alaska with him (except in the comfort of sitting in front of my fire instead of out in the weather). As he said on January 1, 1944:

> *"Still storming--wind and snow--you can't stand up in it, you can't see, and if you stop, you freeze. Lovely weather! A good turkey dinner."*

History is not just a list of dates and a bunch of dead guys, but a series of interwoven stories and events that read like a novel--it isn't until you start putting storylines together that history becomes fun, interesting, exciting. My own children once said "Dad, all the vacations we ever went on had something to do with history." I like to think of it this way, history has something to do with everything.

Reading the journal, I began to wonder about the original journal and its message: If Robert Allen died in 1963, the journal had likely been in this box in the attic on 4th Street in Shelton for 60 years, did he ever share it with anyone after WWII (had anyone read it in 80 years)? With the "Greatest Generation" now almost entirely gone, had people ever experienced what life was like for the soldier in the war stationed in the forgotten front in the Aleutian Islands?

I experienced life in the Aleutians from him. I was able to read about daily life: weather, monotony, living conditions, longing for letters and so much more. My goal in turning his journal into a book was for him to speak to you. I wanted people to experience the "daily" life of the Alaskan soldier during WWII as he experienced it. Experiencing as he did the perseverance & ingenuity, the isolation & commitment. Millions of men and women served. Robert Allen's journal makes it personal.

Introduction

Where are the Aleutians?   The Aleutians are an island chain southwest of Alaska. As Robert Allen recorded in his journal Sept 27 1943, "Looking at a map I see we are almost due west of Seattle.   No wonder we sailed into the sunset each night, on the way up, or out, here." This remote island chain was little known at the time and considered "way up north."   As his ship traveled north & west from San Francisco, he and others speculated where they might be headed.

What happened there prior to the arrival of Robert Allen in Aug 1943?   Author Brian Garfield opens his book *The Thousand-Mile War: World War II in Alaska and the Aleutians* with this : "It is about a thousand miles from Dutch Harbor, near the Alaska Peninsula, to Attu at the far western tip of the Aleutian Island Chain. They are the most brutal thousand miles in the Pacific Ocean.   Here, for fifteen months in 1942-1943, was fought one of the toughest campaigns of World War II." Strategically, both the Americans and the Japanese saw value in these remote islands--for supply stations as well as launching points for aircraft and ships for attacks on one's enemies.   The Japanese attacked islands Kiska & Attu in June of 1942, at the same time as the battle of Midway was going on further south in the Pacific.

It wasn't until April 1943 that American troops were being deployed for the "invasion" of these islands to take them back for America.[1]   Attacks via plane and ships, throughout the terrible weather, continued from May 1943 through August of that year. Brian Garfield details the battles & plans & casualties throughout this time frame.   The invasion of Kiska, the final island occupied (so it was believed) was scheduled on August 15th, 1943.   The "invasion force left Adak on August 13th" (Garfield).   Robert Allen says in his journal that his troop ship left on August 15th from Adak. As it turns out, the Japanese

---

[1] Brian Garfield says in *The Thousand-Mile War* "...every effort was made to keep their destination secret, and only a handful of the division's top officers knew they were going to the Aleutians."

had taken advantage of the weather and evacuated Kiska without the Americans knowing.   The "invasion" took place on August 15th and the "soldiers [were] searching for those caves [where the Japanese were rumored to be hiding] until August 22."   And   "the invasion of Kiska marked the official end of the Aleutian Campaign. After 439 days of warfare, the Chain was scratched off global maps as a combat theater." [2]

Thereafter, the invasion force became an occupying, construction team or as one historian put it the "theater turned into a backwater, garrison troops for the remainder of the war."[3]   Robert Allen records in his journal on September 6 :   "Came ashore Aug 22, and promptly traded our guns for shovels." He literally disembarks on the day that the "invasion" is declared over. Robert Allen details what life is like for a year in this remote area of the globe. Though the "Thousand-Mile War" has ended, the importance to American interests and the

---

[2] Garfield--*Thousand-Mile War.*
[3] Seth Paridon--*Truly Forgotten Fronts*

presence of American troops continue. Robert Allen tells us the rest of the story.

Structure of the Journal. Robert A. Allen's journal begins with him in San Francisco, reporting to a ship for deployment. Though the ship is crowded, we are alone with his thoughts as the ship heads out & he tries to guess the destination.

As he changes location or begins to think/dream about something else, the chapter changes.

All words in the journal are directly from Robert Allen's writing. Anything that I added or defined or clarified, I marked with [brackets]. Items in (parenthesis) are his notations. As much as possible, I used his spelling, his punctuation. Footnotes are added for more historical examples or clarification, with an emphasis on the *Shelton Mason County Journal* to show what the "folks" back home were experiencing at that point.

[Page one of Robert Allen's handwritten journal starts with this notation]

PVT. Robert A. Allen
        July 15 [19]43
                (NOTES of a BOATRIDE)

Ch. 1 Notes of a Boatride--but where to?

July 15

Left Fort Ord with an advance unit from the outfit, early July 17. The Pier[']s in Frisco, and the ship which will be home for now. Aboard immediately and, to work. Unloading convoy trucks, loading the ship, cleaning same (Aegean [sic] Stables)[4]; K.P. for three days--soft--only 100 men to feed,--different now, I think, with troops aboard. Found with dismay no 'Liberty' or shore leave for the troops. Stuck on board.

---

[4] Augean Stables--"For the fifth labor, Eurystheus ordered Hercules to clean up King Augeas' stables. Hercules knew this job would mean getting dirty and smelly, but sometimes even a hero has to do these things."

(Did embezzle my way second night up to Fisherman's Wharf, and got a quart of Brandy--no whiskey to be had, and back on board without mishap). Spent several days being lost, trying to get acquainted with ship--it's big. Frisco Bay is huge and busy.

Have learned our ship U.S.S. Grant, is an oldster of German birth, the former 'Wilhelmina Eugenia Pornoff[5],' or somethin'; was refitted etc, Mare Island [19]27-28.

Troops came aboard night of [July] 21,--it's crowded. My compartment 4D10 (fourth deck down) is about 20 x 20 and sleeps 24 men fairly comfortably. There is really Brass aboard--besides the naval officers, Army men, 2nd Loot's [Lieutenants] to Captains, are knee deep. Majors, Colonels, three Gens, and an Admiral. The Grant is convoy Flagship.

Watched the tugs tie on the evening of 22nd. Went down to chow, came back up on deck to find we were on our own and headed for the Golden Gate.

Wanted to see that bridge but never figured I'd be going under her and headed

____

[5] Originally a German ocean liner named **König Wilhelm II**, she was seized by the United States during the First World War.

out to sea[6]. About two hours out went thru a school of whales, doing their evening calisthentics [original spelling]; Scarcely believable--so big and active and so close in.

The sailors say this big island has a floating speed of fifteen knots. Maybe that's right, but it seems we are moving faster than that. Anyway, I don't think they are pushing her, so we'll say 12 or 13 knots. On a 24hr basis and getting back to miles, the way I figure it we should be about 900 mi[les] out. A funny thing tho[ugh], for the past three evenings, we've been heading almost directly into the sunset. I don't know anything about navigation, but it seems a queer direction to be taking to get to Alaska, where rumor has headed us. My first ride out of sight of land and, whadya know, I'm not sea sick yet. Don't know whether to be disappointed or not. But then the weather is swell and the Ocean is calm as a small lake. So far the Peaceful Blue of the Pacific is an apt description. On the Second night out, all ship's clocks were set back one hour. What could be the reason for that?

---

[6] Completed May 27, 1937, according to Britannica

Whether it is chow, movies, ship's store or almost anything done on board is done by a line. That is, you join a line that might be the length of the ship, and stay in it. If it is the right one it will eventually get you there. But you've got to learn to discriminate--You might climb into what you think is the Chow line and have it slowly but surely take you to the Latrine or any damn place, other than the Mess Hall.

Ship board is worse than camp for rumors.   Been several destinations added, but still don't know where we[`]re going. Seattle? Adak? Kiska? Kodiak? Hawaii?

A.77th 9[?] is s[up]posed to be the biggest force leaving the Coast and I tho[ugh]t ours would be huge convoy, but up to now, no convoy.   Just the Grant and a watchful Destroyer up front.

Today there was a Smoker on board. Improm[p]tu affair--nobody hurt.   Most of the matches between Army and Navy or Marines.   In our first news broadcast (P.A.),

Mussolini takes a powder[7]--Wish all the Enemy was W[**].

Odd how cut off one feels without news papers or radio. Clocks set back an hour again tonight.

Tonight our A.P.O address was posted:

> Pvt. Robert A Allen 39171677
>
> 134th Signal Company A.P.O. #730
>
> C/0 Postmaster Seattle Wash.

--Hmmm--

July 26--Today has been foggy with spots of rain and so I missed the sunset, but think we have shifted North somewhat. Unless I was wrong on the start, we should be about 1400 miles from starting point by now.

My expectations of big Convoy are shot, I guess--just us and our watch dog up forward. More Whales. Wearing a life jacket is natural now. Had to take off our knives (shoulder insignia); now sewing [th]em back on. Large detail maps of Kiska appeared on the walls today. Still have our Sea Gull escort.

---

[7] In July 1943, Italians voted Benito Mussolini out of office. The **Shelton Mason County Journal** reported it this way on July 29th: "The Axis dictator chain is now broken with the passing of the bum Mussolini."

July 28--Hope the man at the wheel isn't as lost as I am. Been in the fog for two days. Damp. Sun has deserted me. Tonight we must be about 2200 miles out.

General Stations (same as an Alert, ashore) sounded this afternoon, but nothing happened--don't know what it was. Ships clocks set back another hour today. Bulletin board says mail will be posted in Adak. So I guess we must touch at Adak.

July 29th--WELL!! What the devil has happened to the Peaceful Blue of the Pacific? Today it has by no means been blue or peaceful. Been acting as tho[ugh] twas mad at sompthin [original spelling] or somebody. And the old boat has been rocking! Chow lines noticeably thinner, and a good many of the boys assuming the 'position'. When he gets his appetite back, I wonder what one poor devil is going to do--his store teeth went overboard with his breakfast today. Not sick as yet, but all day I've had that 'one too many' feeling.

My figures show us to be 2500 miles over from Frisco--some time I'm going to check on that [His math was fairly accurate, as it was likely 2100-2300 miles they traveled]. Word has passed that we are skirting within some miles of land tonight. Too foggy to see. Some of the sailors figure we will touch somewhere, some time tomorrow. Must be some where off the coast of Alaska, but I'll be damned if I know how we could have gotten there. If I'd been steering this thing in the direction where I figured Alaska was, I'd probably be in Texas now. Maybe its just as well I'm in the Army and not the Navy.

Ch. 2 Adak--first step in process

July 30

Early this morning passed a small island. Not long after we were headed into a harbor--It is Adak. Looked out and tho[ugh]t the whole fleet was here--the Convoy. Tied up at 10:00 A.M.

Aug. 12th--Yesterday, came down from the hills of Adak, with 150 lb. packs; loaded on small boats and are again aboard the Grant. Lying out from the island among more ships than I've ever seen before. As I left the dock, waved greetings to about a dozen buddies from the 65th. First time I'd seen [th]em for two months, tho[ugh] I[`]d heard they were on Adak, where we spent twelve days. Most of the time it rained--today the sun is shining! Three days in pup tents, then put up the eight man tents and had a stove to help get dried off. Movie theatres and P.X.s scattered all over the island. Saw a show almost every night. Inexpensive.

Shows 10 [cents]; Cigarettes-50C carton, candy bars three for a dime, etc. No drinks, no women. Did get an occasional glimpse of a few nurses. Met Bud Starr and Tingstead from Shelton[8]. They named nearly a dozen men from there who are working up here. Sea Bees. Didn't see any more of them. Adak is a fairly large collection of hills and mts. Rugged, green and treeless. When the first troops arrived over a year ago, there was nothing but mud and lack of inhabitants. Now--roads everywhere, docks, air fields, installations, and hundreds of thousands of military Personnel.[9] See more planes here than L.A. No Jap[ane]s[e] yet. Casualty list practically nil. One soldier a Pneumonia victim, while several pilots have died in crashes.

Next stop, apparently Kiska--about 200 miles. Don't know how soon we will shove off--maybe another day, week, or what?

---

[8] Robert A. Allen and Roy T. Tingstead mentioned as serving from Mason County in **Shelton Mason County Journal** April 3 1942

[9] Garfield writes almost the same thing more than 25 years later in *The Thousand-Mile Front* "...a year ago [Aug 1942], there had been nobody on the island [Adak]. Now its population was 90,000."

Aug. (Friday 13)--It is evening, and the so called 'fateful day' has passed without incident. However, from the decks of the 'Grant' considerable activity may be seen in the area. Troopships, freighters etc, slowly moving from one anchorage to another. Battleships, like sleepy monsters, seemingly rousing themselves; destroyers prowling about, while the surface is covered by small boats hurrying everywhere. Been reading Kiska data.[10] Seems there are a few misinformed Jap[ane]s[e] there. We shall correct that.

---

[10] In June 10, 1943, the **Shelton Mason County Journal** reported "The details of this flight have not yet appeared in print, but it is apparently a major effort to take over the Aleutians, and we are hearing now of the wiping out of the Jap[anese] on Attu Island and the constant bombarding of Kiska, proving that the enemy is well entrenched and will make a desparate(sic) stand before being wiped out of that part of the U.S.A. in order to 'save face'."

Ch 3 Kiska--meeting the enemy?

Aug 15--Left Adak 6:30 A.M. Kiska tomorrow

Aug. 21--Have been anchored off the Island for several days and it seems, Kiska is ours! Circled the Island all day of the 17th then anchored at the No[orth]. tip under Kiska Volcano. Took off in dense fog, night later, and morning found us one of many ships in the harbor. Bering Sea somewhat different than Pacific. Statement came out a few days past denying Jap[anese] claim of having sunk USS Grant. Slight exaggeration. Have been several 'General Stations' but nothing came of them. Four Jap[anese] ships in the harbor, three beached, and just the mast tips showing of the fourth. Kiska a mountainous strip, 4 to 6 miles wide and 22 long. Fog, rain, wind and a little sunshine; sometimes all at once.

I, not the Jap[ane]s[e], misinformed. Simply not here. Without folding tents, they still had simulated the Arabs. Haven't been on shore detail yet, but will be soon. Fear of mines and 'booby traps' practically dissappated [original spelling], so, many souvenirs have appeared[11] on board. Every object imaginable. Occupation surprisingly bloodless. I wonder, are we pleased or --disappointed? My '03[12] still not fired. Must write home, but there is so little one can say.

Sept 6. Came ashore Aug 22, and promptly traded our guns for shovels. Been busy digging tent locations, stringing wire etc. Not much time for exploring. Island is full of Jap[anese] caves and wrecked houses. This place surely took a beating from the air before we got here. But no Jap[ane]s[e]. Harbor is practically empty of ships and we are Kiska inhabitants.--For how long I wonder? Limited casualties due to mines, grenade carelessness, and one encounter at night between two U.S. units,--bullets really

---

[11] In Robert Allen's journal pages was the postcard pictured later. While he doesn't mention it specifically, it is a "postcard" with an address of a Japanese man. Likely Allen's "souvenir" that survived in his journal for 80 years.
[12] Model 1903 Springfield Rifle

flying. [13] This would be good country for goats--its all uphill, but not even the goats are here. Mud every where, wind and rain. Had three days that might have been borrowed from So. Cal. ; the rest, wet. At times you can actually lean on the wind. Today was a big day. Mail came. All dated in July but surely welcome. Several home town papers,[14] a letter from 'Little Mike' in Colorado Springs, and a couple letters from my Sis, Marg in Seattle. From Adak I wrote Dad and H. McGaughe,--wonder if they got 'em.   Might find time to write some letters soon.

---

[13] According to the Naval History Museum, on August 15, the Allied troops landed, expecting a large force of Japanese to meet them. During the eight-day search, 28 Allied servicemen were killed by friendly fire, along with an additional four killed by Japanese booby traps.   When USS *Abner Read* (DD-526) struck a floating mine on August 17, seventy-one men further died. The island was declared secure on August 24

[14] While it is unclear which specific papers arrived, some headlines from the **Shelton Mason County Journal** dated August 26th, 1943 may have been of interest for him wondering about "home": "News of our Men & Women in Uniform", "Price Ceiling in Effect for Local Stores", "Speaker Tells Kiwanians About Europe", "Call Issued for More USO Hostesses", as well as birth, marriage and death notices.

Sept 27   Been in the Army 18 mo. today, and on Kiska about six weeks. Have missed some days, so will go back: Wouldn't mind this place too much, if it was in the states, if it wasn't so damn windy, rainy, foggy, and muddy. If I could go to town, if I could see a gal, if I could get a drink. There is nuthin' [original spelling]. Looking at a map I see we are almost due west of Seattle. No wonder we sailed into the sunset each night, on the way up, or out, here.

Six men to a tent. Sgt. Budge, P.F.C Baker; P.F.C. Pfarr; Pvt Coon, Pvt Wollert; Pvt Allen, --Construction team. Cots, sleeping bags, coal stove, wooden floor. Work like hell, eat the same way, and sleep at every chance. Salmon running when we came. Fresh fish was good. Got [th]em with clubs, knives, shovels, baskets,--anything. The Bering can be a rough devil. Real wind storm several nights ago.   Next morning, wreckage everywhere on the beaches. Landing barges, life boats, piling etc. There are many graves here, some marked; but saw my first military funeral on Kiska. Detachment of sailors buried one of its men with rifle salute. Empty guns, dud shells, old grenades etc. still dangerous.   Today a Canadian soldier struck a kicked around 'dud' shell with a shovel. No more Canadian.

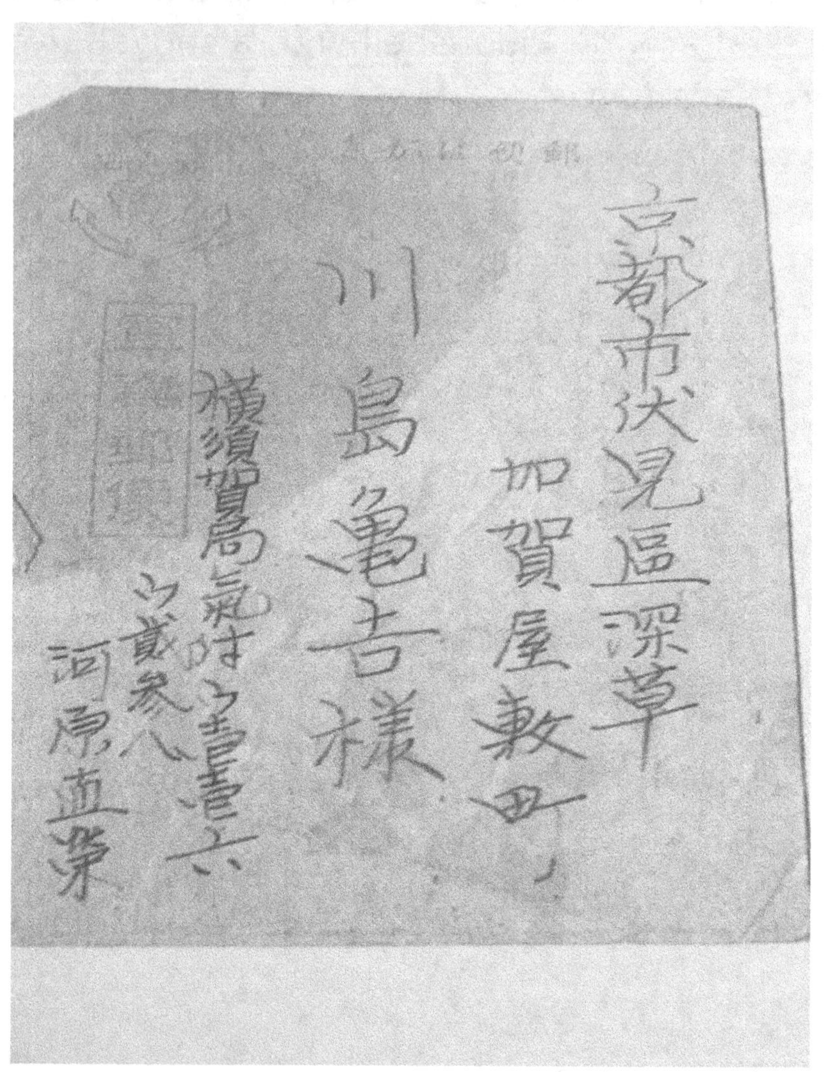

[Found tucked into the pages of his journal. Like a postcard, this apparently gives the name and address of a Japanese soldier, according to a friend who is able to read Japanese]

Ch. 4 Kiska--settling in

Oct 5 Imagine we'll be packing guns with us where ever we go again. 'Tis said we are alerted since Attu was bombed today. Maybe we will have a Nuisance Raid or something. Several days ago a ship came in with a real cargo. Since then we've had fresh meat and vegetables! The team moved to a different area, away from the company, a week ago. Another hill to climb but have a nice tent. Sneaked a hook up on somebody's power line, finally w[r]angled a coupla light bulbs, and we have lights. (That is, sometimes,--they just went out again). Roads are a real problem. If you ever stop piling on rock and sand, the mud will swallow your road in a day. There are some jeeps and trucks but they have been replaced mostly by 'Snowbirds' and Alligators. Snowbird is practically a jeep with treads: Alligator, or water taxi, is an amphib. tank. Dry land, mud or Ocean. American and Canadian equipment (bull-dozers, Cats, Shovels etc), are erasing signs of Jap[anese] occupancy. Looks like some thousands of tents will be replaced by our Ar[c]tic houses (Quonsets). Prebuilt sections piled all over this section. Today we dug fox holes in our area!

Oct 11   Alerted and blacked out tonight. Jap[ane]s[e] were s[up]posed to be over Attu--they must have forgotten somthin' [original spelling] there. This damn rain! I think; twice now had dust on the ground (momentarily), the mud is always knee deep again in a day.

Oct 15   Rumors are flying all over the place as usual, if you listen,--we are leaving any time now. Meanwhile we are digging in sites for Ar[c]tic huts and putting them up as fast as a hole is finished.   Hate to say it, but really believe this is a healthy climate--at least, no flies or mosquitos --you can really sleep. As susceptible as I am to colds, still have nothing more than the old cig(arette) cough.   Censorship regulations tightened. Now there is nothing left of which to write in a letter. Must get hold of the latest list of Cants and Donts. Discouragin'.

Oct 17   This morning the harbor was suddenly alive with craft; 3 transports, ½ dozen destroyers, and smaller Ships. Planes overhead all day.

Oct 24   Coming from that grand State, the Evergreen, I tho[ugh}t I was accustomed to rain.   But this damn stuff up here in the Bering, just isn't civilized. It drives at you all the time carried by a wind which at its gentlest, is a gale. Last night I was sure our tent would take off.   It didn't, but others (untenanted [empty]) were waving in the wind like a frantic washing.   Traffic is practically stopped and our roads which represent weeks and weeks of backbending work, have simply overflowed and gone awandering. Mud everywhere of course, but instead of the usual 6 inches, it is hip deep. Sure fun working.

Oct 27   Snow yesterday and today--and, God help me, I'll take the rain!

Oct 30   Has snowed for three days and Kiska is white. A crust under the snow, but if you break thru, you find mud still underneath.

Nov 2   Wind has swept the snow away--the mud reigns again.   Part of the outfit in section have moved into Pacific Huts. We are still in tent. Have done a lot of work on it. Winterized, but I still expect the wind to pick it up bodily some night, and drop us in a ravine. Pfarr made T/5. When we came on the Island there was a Hell of a lot of Jap[anese] ammo and equipment laying around--now, there is a Hell of a lot of Amer. ammo and equipment laying around.

Nov 11   Armistice Day!![15] Snowing again. What's the matter with me? Still content with being a Pvt. The old urge, or something, isn't there. One of these times, must snap out of it, and gather a few stripes,--at least my own back again. Let's wait awhile yet, tho[ough].

Nov 12 One Pier (dock) completed. Second under way again--held up when they ran into a sunk Jap[anese] sub. Rest of the outfit has

---

[15] Ending of WW1. Was changed to "Veterans Day" in 1954--LOC "this day in history"

moved to area Orderly Room, 1st Sgt., Capt and lackeys. Looks like vacation is over. Rumor has us out of this Godforgot place by the first of the year. Lord God! Would that ever make me unhappy! Many troops have left by boat already. Maybe our turn will come.

Nov 20.   Today was big day. Saw first woman in months.   Nurse off the little transport, "Columbia," tied up for a few days at our dock. She was little, cute and red headed, and came ashore with a five officer escort! Visited in G-4 office while I was installing telephone. Just couldn't seem to get that phone working for a long time. Most of the men of the 134th are from East coast states. Men in my tent from Nor[thern] Cal. Col. NJ. Ohio and Maryland.

Nov 25.   Thanksgiving! Had turkey and 'twas good. And believe it or not, we had the day off. Snow, hail, wind and sleet. Wind keeps snow pretty well swept off, so it isn't much more than 6 in[ches] deep, [ex]cept in the drifts. Can drop out of sight in them.

Nov. 28.   Been snowing for days and everything is frozen. The mud is whipped at last, but I'd hate to be here, when it thaws next summer.   Seeing shows in new mess hall. Pictures are old but good. Xmas pkgs been coming in by the tons.   Folks back home are swell.

Ch. 5 Kiska--longing for a change

Dec 1   Things have been happening--have a new address, and I think 134th is disbanded. We are detached to Alaskan Defense. Pvt. R. A. Allen 39171677 DET. 14th Signal Service Co. A.P.O. 730 Seattle. Looks like I'm in the Aleutians to stay.   States are farther away than ever. Might get off Kiska tho[ugh]. Hope its Kodiak, but prob[ab]ly [i]twill be Attu or some other place as bad as this.

Dec 3   Stopped snowing yesterday; temperature warmed and, today, I'll be damned, if mud isn't boiling [?] thru the ice on our roads! Lordy!

Dec 4   Different ships in harbor, and today Kiska had its 2nd feminine visitor. Also a coupla civilians wandering around. Gal ate dinner in our officer Mess. Who could she be? Blonde, dark skirt, print blouse, and odd colored flesh socks.

Dec 8   Recently completed mess hall torn down to make way for Post theatre. Eating with another outfit. Temporary setup. Rain and wind for two days, and the damn Mud again.   134th is a dead duck. Most of the men will be Detached to 14th, and scattered all thru the Aleutians and Alaska. All moves depending on ship transportation.

Dec 15.   Some shipping lists have appeared. Pfarr--my tent--leaves tomorrow for Attu. I am on the Amchitka list. Not good, but surely better than Kiska. Only 70 miles from here, and an air base.

Dec 16.   Been at Kiska 4 months today, and would be just as pleased if I had never heard of the place. The 'Williwahs'[16] are here, and not friendly. Our work has been finished for some time. Been Trouble Shooting mostly. The life of Riley.

Dec 20   I think winter must be here.

---

[16] "a sudden violent gust of cold land air common along mountainous coasts of high latitudes." --Webster's Dictionary

Dec 24   Xmas Eve!   Had a little Sterno party, and got to harmonizing. That stuff has a bang, and amazing, no head [ache?] afterwards.

Dec 25   Xmas day--Nice dinner--Turkey and a thimbleful of rum--present from the Canadians. Have never seen bad weather till today. All day and tonight it's been whooping it up. The whole damn 'Williwan' family is celebrating at a 100 miles an hour. If the tent doesn't blow away its [be]cause its buried in snow.   Still sweatin' out the Amchitka deal.

Dec 27   Xmas storm has passed. As far as I know only one fatality in this area. Lad from 767 Radar--got lost Xmas Eve. Found him today.

Dec 31   New Years Eve!   We've squeezed island dry of Sterno (canned heat)[17]. At times whiskey can be had, but $60.00 a qt. is kinda high.

---

[17] Alcohol made by soldiers, often called "Torpedo Juice."
--Wikipedia

Jan 1 [19]44   Still storming--wind and snow--you can't stand up in it, you can't see, and if you stop, you freeze. Lovely weather! A good turkey dinner.

[P 28 of the original journal starts with the following notation/"chapter title"?]

<u>Aleutian Incidents</u>
Pvt. Robert A. Allen 39171677
Det. 14th Signal Service Co
A.P.O 730 Kiska

Jan.9 [19]44

    Still 'sweatin out' a boat for Amchitka. Might be a week or a month yet. Most of the Canadians have left the island by now. Some of the men going to Adak, Anchorage etc are s[up]posed to leave this week. Wollert and Ellis (Ellis replaced Baker in team) go to Anchorage, Budge--Amchitka. Coon, to date, stays here. Two men from A Battery 65th, whom I knew, were involved in explosion last week; grenades in coal pile--one dead, one crippled. Weather has been fairly decent for two days, but now [']tis storming again. 'Sterno' has just about disappeared. Soon raisins will be hard to find. About every tent or hut has a five gal. water can of 'Raisin Jack' brewing[18].   Sugar,   yeast,   raisins, lemons,   apples,   potatoes--anything   or everything goes in. Sometimes it brews for as long as 4 or 5 days befor[e] it is drinkable! Nice little brew party a few nights ago. Coupla fistfights etc, but nothing serious. Shooting ducks with army rifles is quite a pastime. So far, we haven't eaten any duck.

Jan 11   Last night and today one of the worst storms yet. Something went wrong with plumbing fixtures: two feet of snow on the floor inside tent and piled up higher than door on outside. Tent tin top got blown out of place and stove had a nest of snow. Our little wooden bath house also sifted full of snow. Ellis and Wollert left this morning. Three of us left in tent. About 100 men boarded ship. Anchorage, Adak, Umnak, Cold Bay etc. Just the Sheymna [Shemya] and Amchitka men left[19]. The tents are to be

---

[18] Another alcoholic concoction made by soldiers. --Aleutian Islands Museum
[19] Original order paper found in the journal pages for January 1944 and pictured later.

taken down--men remaining will move into the Pacific Huts.

Jan 13   Sgt Budge moved out today. Just Coon and me left in tent. Huts are all full--I hope.   Went across the island to the 65th area and spent the night with my old buddies. First time I'd seen some of them since the States. Distilled a batch of 'raisin Jack' and had a nice night--remembering 'way back when.'

Jan 15   Today my kid brother Phil[20] goes up for his Induction in the Army. Wonder if he made it. Still snowing at times but not much wind.

Jan 20   Weather been nice for a week. Moved into a Pacific Hut today.   10 men in this one. Comfortable and out of the weather but believe I'd still take the old tent. Don't have a radio but we get earphone radio programs. I have a field telephone tapped in on a line to a speaker, in another Hut, which in turn is connected to a radio in still another Hut. Sounds involved but works. Everyone

----

[20] Philip Allen, from Shelton, WA.

is making rings from Jap[anese] plane parts etc. Still waiting on transportation to Amchitka.

[Transcript: ALL MEN OF THIS ORGANIZATION LEAVING FOR ANCHORAGE, ADAK, UMNAK, COLD BAY, AND ALL POINTS EAST WITH THE EXCEPTION OF SHEYMNA AND ~~ANCHORAGE~~ AMCHITKA, WILL BE READY TO DEPART AT THE HOUR OF 0930 SHARP ON TUESDAY MORNING. BARRACKS BAGS WILL BE LOADED AT THE TOP OF THE HILL IN THE VICINITY OF OFFICERS QUARTERS. RUCK SACKS WILL BE CARRIED BY THE PERSONNEL.
ALL COTS AND BOMFORTERS[?] WILL BE TURNED INTO THE RADIO REPAIR HUT, HALFWAYS UP THE STAIRS BY ALL PERSONNEL LEAVING AS SOON AS AFTER BREAKFAST AS POSSIBLE ALL PERSONNEL AFTER LOADING THEIR BARRACKS BAGS WILL ASSEMBLE IN THE VICINITY OF THE MESS HALL. THAT'S ALL.

[Original mimeographed order of transfer found in the pages of Robert Allen's hand written journal]

Ch. 6 Amchitka--something new

Feb 3 <u>Amchitka</u>-- A.P.O. #986

    Yesterday we left Kiska--40 of us. 7 hour ride to the new home. Rode in a little old 60 ft. Freight Packet. Sea was rough and everybody was sick. I heaved till there was nothing in me--then kept on heaving. No more rides like that, please. Amchitka is bigger than Kiska, and is flat, with nothing to stop the wind.

Feb 7 I tho[ugh]t we'd gotten here in the middle of a storm, but guess its just ordinary. Does it ever blow! Looks like I drew one of those things--switch board operator! Anyway I guess it beats climbing icy poles in a gale. About 18000 troops on this island at present. Flying base--a fighter strip and a bomber strip. There might be a little bad feeling between the 'native' Signal men and us foreigners from Kiska. We bro[ugh]t a lot of ratings with us. In the Amchitka Detachment the highest rating was Cpl. We bro[ugh]t a 1st Sgt. Their Acting 1st was a Buck. Our

Wire Chief is a M/Sgt.--Acting Chief here was Pvt. Our Master Sgt. is T/Sgt.--he replaced a T/5. Our Telephone Chief is S/Sgt.; Acting chief here was Pvt. And on and on. From Kiska came a T/3; a Buck Sgt.; T/4s and T/5s. Naturally the men who have been here, up to a year, are getting a bad deal, but it just means that those of us without stripes are S.0.S. The day after arriving here, had my first shower/bath in 6 mo[nths], and it was the longest ever.

Feb 8.   Got mail from home today and learned the kid brother, Phil. made the Navy[21] and also got himself married to a widow.[22] He's at Farragut. Was nice today. Almost shirt sleeve weather. We have steel cots, mattresses, pillows and blankets! Chow is not so hot, but maybe the last month at Kiska is at fault,--we really did eat good then. Water here is not as good as there. Have a radio.

---

[21] June 15, 1944 **Shelton Mason County Journal** lists both Robert A. Allen (Army) and Philip L. Allen (Navy) among hundreds of others under the headline "Mason County Honor Roll" as WWII participants

[22] Philip L Allen married Madelene Zornes in Seattle, WA on January 20, 1944 according to Marriage Certificate--family research from Ancestry.com

Feb 15   Weather has warmed up some and there is plenty water from melting snow. T/3 Lansford (Radio) starts for the States today on special assignment.   He came from the States with us.   Men in this hut are from Minn., Ore., Florida, Okla., Mo., Tenn., Mass., R.I., Mich. and Wisc.

Feb. 20   Had two drinks of real whiskey --first since the States.   It can be had,--$70.00 a qt.   A[c]quired by theft, raisins and sugar--have a can of 'Jack' set. Much shipping in the harbor.   And air mail service is good.

Feb 26   Weather has warmed up some, and except for occasional wind storms, it isn't bad.   More hours of day light.   I am afraid this island will be nothing but mud when the ground thaws.

Mar 3   Been pretty lucky at poker for a while but last night,--got hot in a wild game and made biggest winning yet--$960.00 and a good wrist watch.[23]

Mar 6   Three transports in today, including U.S.S. Grant, first time she's been up since we rode her in July.   Black out last night. Olivia De Havilland[24] made an unskeduled [original spelling] visit to the Island.   She was a guest at our radio station W.X.L.K. Didn't see her.

Mar. 11   Most of the snow is gone.   Wind, sleet.   Got a 'Coke' ration last week, 12 bottles.   Bought a Rx. wrist watch $22.00. There are prob[ab]ly a number of casualties we never hear about.   Accidental gunfire etc. Last night a lad was drowned;   while another got a broken leg in a road accident.

---

[23] According to Brian Garfield in *The Thousand-Mile War*, "Poker games were monumental, classic & established in perpetuity."

[24] British actress, played in Gone with the wind in 1939 https://www.imdb.com/name/nm0000014/ , visited the Aleutians in March 1944 on a USO tour.   Mentioned not only in Robert Allen's journal, but those of other soldiers at the time https://www.nps.gov/aleu/learn/photosmultimedia/upload/Aleutians-Carnes-all-508.pdf

Mar 15   Wind and rain Storm almost every day.   Each man got a case of beer for [$]2.40. We get it 8 bottles at a time.   I wrangled 2 ½ cases so I got 20 bottles (Blue Ribbon). And good!

Mar 20.   Second round of beer today. (Schlitz). Harry Wilson, a big fund lovin' boy from Georgia, and I went down to the dock and from a sailor, got 2 qts. Of Rum for 90 bucks.   We'd gotten a qt. Rum once before for $60.00; and 3 qts. Whiskey for $150.00. Kinda high.

Mar 27. My G.d. birthday. Two years in the Army. I was a civilian; then Pvt; then Cpl.; then Pvt. to complete the circle, I'd like to be a civilian again. Wilson and I went up to the Radio Sta. WXLK. A party,--alcohol and beer. Nice bunch of boys there.

Mar 30   Mud! Mud! Mud! It's sure sticky. Snowed for a coupla days but it doesn't stay put. Have been digging out around the Hut and putting up a sand bag wall--protection, camouflage--and,   a   conditioner   [?].

Something seems to be stirring but I don't know what.

Apr 5   Rec. Hall #1, a large building in our area, burnt to the ground today.   Most effective thing on a half dozen fire trucks was the sirens.   You can't put out a fire with noise.

Ch. 7 Amchitka--winter fading

Apr. 10   Been nice weather for almost a week. Sun's been out and the days are long. Gets light about 6A.M.--night doesn't come till about 10P.M. Those sandbags will get me.

Apr. 22   Sun is almost warm and the ground is dry--had a snow storm right in the middle of a sunshiny day. Amchitka is 35 mi[les] x 23 mi[les] and the island Personnel is steadily being cut down. Figure on about 10,000 Army, besides the Navy complement. Bringing a flock of civilians in tho[ugh]--several thousand of them here now. A lot of projects including concrete runways on the Strips.

Apr 27 Foggy and wet for a week. Sand bagging about done, and the C.O. says a good job done. The kid brother left Cal. today for the So. Pacific. And the brother-in-law arrives in Hawaii[25]. Heard a

---

[25] George Cardinal--according to **Shelton Mason County Journal** of December 2, 1943--"Pvt George Cardinal, former Rayonier employee, is now stationed in Camp Roberts Calif,

nurse's voice on the phone and didn't sleep for three nights! We have an 'in' on the liquor problem--get it cheaper but it's still too high (about [$] 35.00 a qt.). Have to quit it--it's been soaking up all my winnings.

May 10   Rec. Hall #1 rebuilt. Gym and movies. Half a dozen movie houses--late pictures. Also softball, smokers etc.

May 15 Weather kinda soggy. Have seen quite a few of the fellows from 65th. Stopping here on way to other posts. One Emergency Furlough, two fellows going to school in Seattle; several going to Adak for W.O. Exam. Some fellows here from the old 134th in Kiska, going to Richardson [Anchorage Base]. Ted Coon broke a leg.

May 20 Many men from different units going to the States on Rotation (24 mos. or over). And many more sweatin' out a furlough--12 to 18 mos. Up here--I still got 2 mos. to go, to be eligible for the bottom of the list. Soft living isn't going to get me down but will get

---

with an infantry outfit. His wife Dorothy and daughter Sandra Ann are living in Shelton." [Sandra was my mother]

me fat. Weigh 192! Work 5 ½ hours a day with a day off each week.

June 1	Four more men from the 14th left today on Furlough. Casserio from my Hut goes to Rhode Island. New hospital has health hut--showers, steam bath, sun lamp etc. Really all neat. Cigs. went up .05--.50 c a carton.

June 6.	Last night Invasion news came thru the board at 9:50P.M[26]. And tonight at least three Generals with their staff arrived by plane [to?] Amchitka.

June 20	Foggy and windy. Four men from 14th transferred to Mainland. One of them is Davis from my Hut. Issued sheets today.

June 25	Letter from my kid brother in the Admiralities [original spelling]. An Infantry Lt. killed in a cave-in. Big funeral. Our ex

---

[26] D-Day--**Shelton Mason County Journal** of June 8, 1944--"...news of the invasion of France...but today the hearts of all America are stilled in anxious waiting for the next hour and day, praying for the success of the Allies and the final destruction of the enemy; the end of war and the return of our boys."

C.O. Capt. Kearny is gone on Rotation. Capt. Campbell takes over. New mess hall opens

June 28, it's a big place. Trays and silver ware so I can put away the beat up old mess kit. Another shot in the arm. Harbor is busy with several ships in. Road crews are working night and day on the roads.

Ch.8 Amchitka--longing for home

July 1   My birthday!   Furlong fever has broken out again--four of our men, gone for 2 months, got back and four or five more are listed to go. Wilson is one of them.

July 10   Foggy and damp.   No visibility for the planes, and little mail. What happened to the 4th of July?   Buster the Co. hound got killed today--he was no match for a jeep. Poor old Buster, he was big footed, awkward and dumb, but he was company. We nursed him thru distemper and other crisises [original spelling] but he just wouldn't stay off the roads.

July 13 Betty, the smart Co. bitch had pups today--11 of them! And Buster was there! Of course he doesn't get all the credit but some of the pups were his. No boats in and Wilson and the boys are still sweatin'.

July 17   Seem to be cutting the Det[ail]. Several days ago 4 men were transferred to Kiska; today 5 more went to Shemnya--two of these were Bell and Erlandson who came from the States with us. Among the people I like best is my Hut member, little rosy-cheeked Chuck Hewins from Penn. He has been with me since the States. Just turned 21, and has 7 brothers in the Service.

July 19   Rain and wind.[27] Most everyone has a cold--must be the fog. Wilson, Webb, Coleman and Reagan still sweatin' out furlough transportation.

July 22   Rain has stopped but the wind is blowing like hell. Today I am 1 year gone from the States.   They are asking for Paratroop volunteers. Quite a number have signed up from here. I am too heavy, too old and without the inclination.   Tojo has apparently quit and it seems, some one

---

[27] Another Shelton soldier, Pvt. Don Philips, stationed in the Aleutians, wrote a letter to the **Shelton Mason County Journal,** published July 20, 1944 & also talked about the weather: "One of our worst handicaps is the weather. The summer is no better than the winter at home and the wind in the winter is unbelievable."

mislaid an egg for Hitler[28].   Coleman of telephone maintenance left by plane July 20. Furlough takes him to Okla.

July 24 Sun has been up and it's actually warm!   A bomber came in with fighter escort--that means a load of brass.   Wilson left yesterday by plane, starting his furlough in Covington, Georgia.   It will be lonesome here for a coupla [original spelling] months without the big lug. ($100.00) [$ Reference unclear?]

July 27   Sgt. Webb of the line crew left on Furlough to Tenn.   July 24.   Reagan also to Tenn. left today.   A boat came in tonight bringing 5 furlough men back.   Casserio among them.   The boys say the States are pretty swell but expensive as all hell.

Aug. 2   July has passed, leaving us with mud and fog.   A new deal is on with furloughs.   All men with 12 months up here are eligible for the drawings till their 18th mo. (rotation time) is passed.   That makes

---

[28] Operation Valkyrie--assassination attempt against Hitler on July 20th, 1944 was unsuccessful.

about 50 of us. At each drawing 5 names will be drawn out of the hat. How lucky am I? From the So. Pacific--kid brother gets a broken arm from a fall from a cliff. For some time now the tundra grass has become greener and a few odd looking wild flowers appeared briefly. Days are getting much shorter and it looks as tho[ugh] we can prepare for another winter. Weather been bad and little mail has arrived. For me--practically none. Amchitka really isn't flat--a series of low hills and valleys and small lakes. But the lowest spot on Kiska, a pass 300 ft above S[ea] L[evel], is prob[ab]ly higher than any place here. S[up]posed to go on the range today (Carbines) but twas too rough.

Aug 10 No mail from home for a long time. Furloughs depend entirely on transportation. On the draw, only two men got out, by boat--Newberry to Texas and Gadowski to Ohio. F.D.R spent several days in Adak,[29] the

---

[29] According to the **Anchorage Daily News**, 70 years later in 2014 commemorating the visit, FDR said at the time "We are all doing a great deal to make it impossible for them [the Japanese] to repeat this particular route of access to the

military capital of the Aleutians. There is s[up]posed to be (according to rumor) a Task force training on Adak. Operators are working longer hours now. From 5 to 6 hrs.; now it's 8 hrs a day. The new C.O. is inclined to be G.d. and figures (prob[ab]ly nightly) the men dont have enough to do. Inspections are coming more regularly--the next thing you know we'll be saluting the officers! One rumor, at least, is about to come true. The detachment here is going to be cut about in half--men will go to Aleut[ian] posts. Don't know what's in store for me. Ratings are damn tough to get up here--I've been in too many outfits and had too many different jobs to get a start on the Non. Com ladder again.

Aug 15   A group of nurses made landing on the island today! Have heard some of their voices on the phone but haven't seen 'em yet.   They are not for us tho[ugh]--the officers are greater wolves than the men and are in better positions to get their neglected home work done. I don't believe anyone, up

---

United States. That is why it is important, this work we are all doing on this spot."

here for a year or more, will fully escape the ravages of rheumatism, arthritis, sompthin [original spelling].   Rain and wind and fog thru Aug.

Aug. 20   U.S.O. Show Troup #257 on the island--3 gals and 4 guys. Pretty good show. Officers are really giving the nurses a run. Some of those gals are dated up for two weeks ahead. It's 'agin' [against] the rules, of course, but sweatin' out the officer-nurse phone calls on the switchboard is fun. Vicarious romancing maybe, and prob[ab]ly moronic but, what the hell! At first, just the sound of a female voice on the phone would set the exchange in a dither. Several of them are young and cute, but they all look good to me. Perfume!

Aug 30   Weather wet and sticky--the wind is something too to give you nightmares. Military funeral today for a lad who was drowned several days ago--fishing. No wild life of any kind on the Rock but the water is teeming with fish of all sizes and descriptions. Never seen such trout.

Ch. 9 Amchitka--heading home on furlough

<u>Sept 1</u>   It has really happened! 2 names were drawn from the furlough hat; Cpl Fuller's from Ind. and,--MINE!! Boy! OH Boy! No plane transportation available, so I'll be on the little transport "Chisikoff" when it leaves Sept 5th or 6th. Am I lucky!!

Sept 3   Funeral today for a Major who was killed in a plane crash on Kiska. He and another officer left here with a coupla nurses on an unauthorized joy-ride.

Sept 4   My boat came in this morning with a lot of replacements. Coleman and Butler. I'll be on it, 6th, maybe.

Sept 6   Hit the gangplank 16:30; under way 1700. Transport is small and loaded. About 1100 troops--unit rotation, some casuals (furloughs) and civilian workers. Two escort ships, destroyer and sub. chaser picked us up out side of the harbor.

Sept 7   Anchored off Adak 0900. Will dock this aft[ernoon]. for more troops. One more stop I think--Dutch Harbor. Should make Seattle 17th or 18th. Left Adak 19:30. Picked up about 500 more troops. Chow lines are rugged. Stand up to eat.

Sept 10   Patches of snow still on some mts. Passed a lone whale and a smoking volcano. Bunks are racked up like shelves in a cupboard--sleep head to foot and elbow to elbow. Had sunshine first two days. Last night the old tub was pitching and bucking. Mount your bunk going by and hang on! Yesterday, anchored momentarily at D[utch] H[arbor]--clearance papers--and we're on our way!

Sept 13   Escort ships left us a coupla days ago. Its been fairly nice since we've been in Pacific waters--I must be a good sailor, not sea-sick yet. Should be in Seattle Fri. night or Sat. morning. 17 day furlough! Won't be back in the Aleutians for about 2 months.

Will I ever hate to come back! Have gained back 2 hrs. Of the 3 we lost 14 mos. ago.

Sept 15   (afternoon) Listened to a Portland brdct [broadcast?] last night and caught up with P.C. time. Tho[ugh]t we'd see land today but there is nothing but fog and rain. Must be approaching the Sound. Using the whistle as a fog horn. Dock in the morning

[Allen's journal ends there. He was almost home. After landing in Seattle, he would need to find his way to Shelton. Though many blank pages remained in tablet that he was writing on, those pages remained blank]

Bibliography

"Allied Invasion of Kiska." *National Museum of the U.S. Navy*, Navy History and Heritage Command, www.history.navy.mil/content/history/museums/nmusn/explore/photography/wwii/wwii-pacific/aleutian-islands-campaign/allied-invasion-kiska.html#:~:text=Following%20the%20Battle%20of%20Attu,under%20deep%20fog%20and%20darknness. Accessed 10 June 2024.

"The Augean Stables Hercules Cleans Up." *Hercules' Fifth Labor: The Augean Stables*, Perseus Project, www.perseus.tufts.edu/Herakles/stables.html. Accessed 10 June 2024.

Budge, Kent G. "Alcohol." *The Pacific War Online Encyclopedia: Alcohol*, 2013, pwencycl.kgbudge.com/A/l/Alcohol.htm.

Carnes, Frank F. "Memories of the Aleutians Campaign, WWII." *National Parks Service Aleutian Memories*, NPS.gov, www.nps.gov/aleu/learn/photosmultimedia/upload/Aleutians-Carnes-all-508.pdf. Accessed 10 June 2024.

Garfield, Brian. *The Thousand-Mile War: World War II in Alaska and the Aleutians*. 2nd Printing July 1971 ed., Ballantine Books, 1971.

"Golden Gate Bridge." *Encyclopædia Britannica*, Encyclopædia Britannica, inc., 23 May 2024, www.britannica.com/topic/Golden-Gate-Bridge.

IMDb. "Olivia de Havilland | Actress, Soundtrack." *IMDb*, IMDb.com, www.imdb.com/name/nm0000014/. Accessed 10 June 2024.

"Kiwanians Hear Talk By Navy Man." Edited by Grant C Angle, *Shelton Mason County Journal Newspaper Archive*, 10 June 1943, smc.stparchive.com/Archive/SMC/SMC06101943P01.php?tags=kiska%7C1943.

"Marriage Certificate." *Ancestry®*, 18 Jan. 1944, www.ancestry.com/imageviewer/collections/2378/images/84259353_b593ceee-1d1f-4612-a5a9-2816d7849393?pId=839241.

Marriage Certificate from King County, Washington, accessed through Washington, U.S., Marriage Records, 1854-2013 on Ancestry.com

"Mason County Honor Roll." Edited by Grant C Angle, *Shelton Mason County Journal Newspaper Archive*, 15 June 1944,

smc.stparchive.com/Archive/SMC/SMC06
151944P05.php.

"Mason County's Honor Roll." Edited by Grant C Angle, *Shelton Mason County Journal Newspaper Archive*, 4 Apr. 1942, smc.stparchive.com/Archive/SMC/SMC04 031942P02.php?tags=tingstead.

Miskimon, Christopher. "The 1903 Springfield Rifle's Storied Military History." *Warfare History Network*, 16 Sept. 2022, warfarehistorynetwork.com/article/the-1 903-springfield-rifles-stories-military-hist ory/.

"News of Our Men & Women in Uniform--In California." Edited by Grant C Angle, *Shelton Mason County Journal Newspaper Archive*, 2 Dec. 1943, smc.stparchive.com/Archive/SMC/SMC12 021943P08.php?tags=george+cardinal.

"News of Our Men & Women in Uniform." Edited by Grant C Angle, *Shelton Mason County Journal Newspaper Archive*, 26 Aug. 1943, smc.stparchive.com/Archive/SMC/SMC08261943P01.php?tags=august%7C1943.

"On the Way Out of War." Edited by Grant C Angle, *Shelton Mason County Journal Newspaper Archive*, 8 June 1944, smc.stparchive.com/Archive/SMC/SMC06081944P03.php?tags=european%7Cinvasion%7Cjune%7C1944.

"One Dictator Hunts His Role." Edited by Grant C Angle, *Shelton Mason County Journal Newspaper Archive*, 29 July 1943, smc.stparchive.com/Archive/SMC/SMC07291943P06.php?tags=mussolini#google_vignette.

Palek, Stephanie. "Operation Valkyrie 1944." *Cambridge University Library*, 27

Apr. 2015, www.lib.cam.ac.uk/collections/departme nts/germanic-collections/about-collection s/spotlight-archive/operation-valkyrie.

Paridon, Seth. "The Thousand Mile War-the Campaign in the Aleutians with Guest Co-Host Jon Parshall -Episode 222:" *YouTube*, YouTube, 25 July 2023, www.youtube.com/watch?v=qgoWSABsI TU.

Porco, Peter. "When the President Came to Dinner: FDR in Alaska." *Anchorage Daily News*, Anchorage Daily News, 28 Sept. 2016, www.adn.com/culture/article/fdr-alaska/ 2014/09/12/.

"Service News--PVT. Don Phillips Writes from Alaska." Edited by Grant C Angle, *Shelton Mason County Journal Newspaper Archive*, 20 July 1944, smc.stparchive.com/Archive/SMC/SMC07 201944P04.php?tags=aleutian.

"Today in History - November 11." *The Library of Congress*, www.loc.gov/item/today-in-history/november-11/#:~:text=After%20World%20War%20II%2C%20the,call%20the%20holiday%20Remembrance%20Day. Accessed 10 June 2024.

"Torpedo Juice." *Wikipedia*, Wikimedia Foundation, 14 Feb. 2024, en.wikipedia.org/wiki/Torpedo_juice.

"USS U. S. Grant." *Wikipedia*, Wikimedia Foundation, 4 Nov. 2023, en.wikipedia.org/wiki/USS_U._S._Grant.

"Williwaw Definition & Meaning." *Merriam-Webster*, Merriam-Webster, www.merriam-webster.com/dictionary/williwaw. Accessed 10 June 2024.